Methuen Playscripts

The Methuen Playscripts series exists to
extend the range of plays in print by
publishing work which is not yet widely
known but which has already earned a
place in the acting repertoire of the
modern theatre.

Owners

The presentation at the Royal Court's Theatre
Upstairs of Owners, the first stage play by
a young woman playwright who has already
had a number of plays broadcast on radio
and television, was widely interpreted as
signalling the arrival in the theatre of an
exciting and promising talent. Set in an
up-and-coming area of London, Owners is
about a successful property developer who
pursues the man she wants almost as
passionately as she buys up old houses and
drives out the sitting tenants.

Martin Esslin in Plays and Players commented
that Miss Churchill is 'one of the best play-
wrights now active in this country... What
is remarkable is that this play which has
such deep undertones is on the surface a
highly amusing folk-comedy, full of
brilliant observation, witty lines, a truly
Dickensian zest in creating richly eccentric
characters and a wealth of telling theatrical
images. '

OWNERS

CARYL CHURCHILL

First published in Great Britain in 1973
by Eyre Methuen Ltd
11 New Fetter Lane London EC4P 4EE
Copyright ©1973 by Caryl Churchill

Set by Expression Printers Ltd
Printed in Great Britain by
Fletcher & Son Ltd, Norwich

SBN 413 30400 0 Hardback
    413 30410 8 Paperback

Onward Christian Soldiers,
Marching as to war.

> Christian hymn.

Sitting quietly, doing nothing.
Spring comes and the grass grows by itself.

> Zen poem.

<u>Owners</u> was first presented by the Theatre Upstairs at the Royal Court Theatre on 6 December 1972 with the following cast:

CLEGG	David Swift
WORSELY	Richard O'Callaghan
MARION	Stephanie Bidmead
LISA	Anne Raitt
ALEC	Kenneth Cranham
ALEC'S MOTHER	Eileen Devlin
MRS ARLINGTON	Lucinda Curtis
Two Customers	

Directed by Nicholas Wright
Designed by Di Seymour

Marion was played by Jill Bennett in the previews. She was injured and the part was taken over by Stephanie Bidmead.

CLEGG is dowdy and getting fat. He's unattractive but not so grotesquely that it's impossible to imagine Marion having married him when he was younger. Forty.

WORSELY is tall and thin, with greasy black hair, not long; dark blue suit; shiny black pointed shoes. Early twenties.

MARION is thin and edgy and moves about a lot, often eating. Strong face rather than pretty. Her clothes are expensive but often badly matched, coming undone, slightly askew. Thirties.

LISA has a weak pretty face losing its prettiness with strain. When dressed up her hair, eyes and clothes are elaborate: other times it is all let go. At the beginning of the play she is six months pregnant. Late twenties.

ALEC is tall, rather plain and ordinary, but attractive. Thirties.

ALEC'S MOTHER is senile.

MRS ARLINGTON is very young, well dressed, well bred, with the good nature of someone who has never met difficulties or been disliked. No need to send her up – she can be as nice as possible and still be intolerable to Lisa. About twenty.

CUSTOMERS can be any age and can be played by the same actress, but as two different customers, not one.

List of Scenes

The play takes place in a developing bit of North London.

Act One

Inside Clegg's butcher's shop. CLEGG and CUSTOMER.

CLEGG: Lovely day dear. Been sitting in the park in the sun? I know you ladies. Twelve ounces of mince. And what else? Some nice rump steak dear? You don't keep a man with mince. No? Twenty p, thank you very much. Bye-bye dear, mind how you go.

(She goes.)

Old cow.

(He starts chopping chops. WORSELY comes in. His wrists are bandaged.)

WORSELY: Give us a chop.

CLEGG: Have six if you like for the price. It's the last day. Marion tell you?

WORSELY: Said you was closing down. Pongs a bit.

CLEGG: Old stock. I can let you have some kidneys.

WORSELY: I don't go for offal. It's too much like insides.

CLEGG: Nice rabbit?

WORSELY: Rabbit's one of those things I think of you know as a rabbit. Horse the same but the French manage it all right. A nice lamb chop though is definitely a dish.

CLEGG: Have ten.

WORSELY: Aren't they a bit grey?

CLEGG: Lamb always smells a bit strong. You don't want to mind the smell. Run them under the cold tap when you get home.

WORSELY: I like lambs in a field mind you in the spring time. I had quite a pet lamb one holiday when I was a kiddy.

CLEGG: Marion still in the office is she?

WORSELY: Hard for a child till it gets the knack. If the lamb's a pet don't hurt it. If the lamb's a chop, it's not got a name.

CLEGG: Marion very busy I suppose?

WORSELY: Waiting for a big phone call. She's got two buyers after them three houses in a row in the square. Playing them off sort of thing.

CLEGG: One thousand five hundred and seventy five people die daily in England and Wales.

WORSELY: Fair number.

CLEGG: It's only a matter of making her one of them.

WORSELY: It's not so easy. Speaking as one who knows.

CLEGG: She's physically a very strong woman. And mentally in some respects.

WORSELY: But you weren't thinking of unarmed combat?

CLEGG: She did karate once in an evening class. When she had more time on her hands. No I must find the right tool for the job.

WORSELY: Is the idea to kill her at all costs or do you count on getting away with it?

CLEGG: I hadn't planned on being caught, no.

WORSELY: Then a knife might be too much of a clue.

CLEGG: What I'd prefer is a convenient accident. If she could topple off a cliff.

WORSELY: A day trip.

CLEGG: You could come with us as a witness.

WORSELY: A witness is what you don't want.

CLEGG: To say you saw me not push her. An accident.

WORSELY: Are you serious?

CLEGG: How do I know? I know I dwell on murder day and night. I can't see any life for myself till she's gone. And she's in much better health than I am.

WORSELY: Why not leave her?

CLEGG: I tried that once. But where would I go? And she didn't mind at all. Hardly. Not enough. She can stand on her own two feet which is something I abominate in a woman. Added to which she has what you might call a magnetic personality. We got that out of a machine once

on a pier in happier times that said your character. It was
so like it made you wonder just what is above. My card
said exactly the same as hers, which was a mistake on
the part of whoever filled the machine, so I don't know my
true character. But she's a magnet all right. I gather
round. So do you. You kept dropping in all the time till
she said you could work for her and now you work for her
all day and half the night and you still drop in. You're
drawn in. What for? Just to be there when she's there.
You see?

WORSELY: Aren't you afraid I'll tell her?

CLEGG: I have to talk to somebody now and then. I'm very
fond of the dog mind you.

WORSELY: Are you getting another job?

CLEGG: I've been a butcher twenty-five years. And my father
before me. He killed his own meat. Not in London, there
isn't the opportunity, we had the good luck to live in a
suburb that had a small field adjoining the shop. Then we
moved here. It seemed like progress at the time. But now
it's all done by machine a lot of the dignity's gone out of
it. But you still don't see a lady butcher. Apart from the
physical weakness a lady has a squeamishness which is
very proper in the fair sex but shameful in a man. We
were taught to look up to my father. My mother literally
worshipped him. I've seen her on her knees. And he would
raise her up, very gracious. She knew how to give a man
the right support. He had his chair. The tea was hot on the
table when he came in. We never made a sound.

WORSELY: It was Sainsbury's opening next to you did it was
it?

CLEGG: I don't know why people want meat in polythene. It's
like going round with your head in a plastic bag.

WORSELY: You could get another shop better placed. Wouldn't
Marion buy you a shop?

CLEGG: I don't let her buy me a drink. I was going to be big
myself, you don't seem to realize. That was my intention
as a young man. I had none of your difficulties Worsely.
I was thrusting. I envisaged a chain. Clegg and Son. I
was still the son at the time. I would have liked a son
myself once I was the Clegg. But now I've no business I
don't need a son. Having no son I don't need a business.

WORSELY: You need a hobby. Have you no interests?

CLEGG: I could have any number.

WORSELY: Pick one or two and throw yourself in whole-heartedly. You need to keep busy.

CLEGG: I've always been my best under pressure. I thrive on competition. I put two men out of business when I was only twenty-seven years old.

WORSELY: That's where we differ. The slightest pressure from outside and I fall in. Because inside me there is very nearly a vacuum. The balance is just so. I was top in the lower forms of the grammar school. I liked marks then. I sometimes look around now to be marked. Or I mark myself. (He looks at his bandaged wrists.) B minus. Could have tried harder.

CLEGG: Isn't it painful cutting yourself like that? I know when I have the odd slip with a knife I don't half give a yell.

WORSELY: An accident makes you feel got at. If you mean it, the pain's more on your side. Because nobody dies without discomfort. I take it as an occupational hazard. You don't get anything of value without working for it, as the headmaster liked to say at assembly. Per ardua ad astra.

CLEGG: But do you intend to be dead?

WORSELY: I try to. My doctor says I'm so safety prone I must have a lifewish. I have a sense of humour about psychia-
.trists.

CLEGG: I've every respect myself for the mental profession. When Marion was in hospital they tried to tell her she'd be happier and more sane as a good wife. Comb your hair and take an interest in your husband's work. Find a hobby. She had her painting, which was all right. Creative hobbies are very nice for a woman. I appreciate anything pretty and artistic. But she wouldn't listen. She came out of there with staring eyes and three weeks later she bought her first house. It was only fifteen hundred pounds. She had five hundred left her by her dad. And I did the rest for her on a mortgage because the mortgage company was understandably reluctant to deal with a lady. She's paid me back since of course. I would have lost the money gladly and forgiven her and not said another word about it if only she would have stayed with painting and been content.

Everything I had was hers. I always said. She only had to ask.

WORSELY: I was sorry she didn't stay in hospital longer. I used to dance with her at the socials.

CLEGG: Mental hospitals aren't altogether moral. That's the one fault I find. They don't care if what a patient does is good or bad, just if it's good for her or bad for her. Dancing can be very dangerous if it's not watched.

WORSELY: I wouldn't say she danced with everyone. She's not everyone's type.

CLEGG: That I put up with this sort of talk. Or seem to. In fact I bide my time. If I thought for a moment she had dishonoured me, then without hesitation or a thought of the police − (He plunges knife into meat.) And also into the heart of the thief. I am more an Othello than a Hamlet. Out out damned candle! She is legally mine. And one day she will die knowing it. And another satisfaction of my shame is the proof that it's she who is infertile.

WORSELY: But Marion's on the pill. I daresay.

CLEGG: I would never give my name to another man's child. He would be robbing me not only of my helpmate but my chain of highclass butcheries. Clegg and Son. Pork butcher. Clegg and Son. Family butcher. But still she's Mrs Clegg. I am even proud of her. I look at her sometimes and think I am the one this powerful rich property developer swore before God to honour and obey. Whether she does or not. You won't deny she is a wonder. It's very like having a talking dog, and it's on the front page at breakfast, the radio at dinner, the television at night − that's mine, look, that's my clever dog. But a time comes when you say, Heel. Home. Lie down.

WORSELY: You know what you were saying about a plastic bag. Suppose I put a plastic bag over my head and tied it tightly round the neck. What could possibly go wrong?

CLEGG: Some of them nowadays has safety holes.

WORSELY: Not all. I would have a look.

CLEGG: There couldn't be any possible situation in which Marion might put her head in a plastic bag?

WORSELY: Clegg you have no experience of taking life.

CLEGG: I get my ideas mainly from books. I can't ever put

Agatha Christie down. And newspapers are great fun too. But people do die in real life. Daily. In large numbers.

WORSELY: I've tried to kill myself six times. And I'm a willing victim.

CLEGG: I know it's one thing to think about it. When I see her in real life I'm always surprised at the bloom of health.

WORSELY: I saw a poster saying Suicide – ring the Samaritans. So this very pleasant young fellow came round and I told him I want to kill myself and could he help. He said in a very feeling voice he would certainly try. But does he hell. The bastard's always trying to stop me.

CLEGG: It's half past five. Time to close. There should be some ceremony to help. As a funeral does.

(MARION comes in.)

MARION: One hundred thousand.

WORSELY: That's it.

MARION: I held out.

WORSELY: I knew you would.

MARION: I admitted there was competition.

WORSELY: Made him jump.

MARION: I gave him a deadline.

WORSELY: Put him on the spot.

MARION: He came through on the telephone like a lamb. He could after all see his way clear.

WORSELY: Should have asked a hundred and twenty.

MARION: No dear I should not. It was worth perhaps eighty. Don't show off.

CLEGG: Congratulations my love.

MARION: We shall celebrate. It stinks in here, Clegg. Does it always? No wonder you've no customers. Throw it all away. Shut the shop. Whatever's that you're clutching, Worsely? Meat? You won't want it, you'll eat out with us. Chuck it in the bin. What about the rest of it, Clegg? Will you pay the dustmen to take it away? I think I'm turning into a vegetarian.

(Pause.)

I know very well it's a sad moment, I can't be a failure just
to help. We will all go out together and celebrate. Com-
memorate. Make an occasion.

SCENE TWO

Alec and Lisa's room. A lot of furniture in a small space.
Bed stripped, chair overturned, drawers pulled out, clothes
on floor, china smashed.

ALEC is sitting in the armchair, unconcerned. LISA is
rummaging among the clothes on the floor. She's about six
months pregnant. She's dressed up, as they've been out for
the evening.

LISA: What's gone? They've taken the transistor. Have they?
Where did you leave it? They have taken it. They didn't
have to smash the bambi. Oh, oh no, yes, the ring. My
engagement ring. I took it off to do the washing and left it
- unless it fell down. (She rummages among clothes on
the floor, tossing them aside with distaste.) Help me look.
I can't ever have another one. It's my one and only
engagement ring and it's gone. And what else? Try and
look around. Here's the tin had the housekeeping in it.
And where's the clock? I'll be lost in the morning. Oh
Alec get the police, get it all back. Run out to the phone.

ALEC: Let's not get the police, Lisa.

LISA: If we're very quick they might just catch them.

ALEC: I wouldn't want them caught.

LISA: What is it now?

ALEC: If he wants the things that much, perhaps let him have
them.

LISA: I want the things very much. And they're mine.

ALEC: If you have the police you've all the bother. You may
not get anything back. I don't want them catching somebody
for me.

LISA: If we'd come in when he was still here, you wouldn't
have grabbed him.

ALEC: No.

LISA: If we'd found him murdering the boys you'd have stood
there.

(Pause.)

I'm going to get the police.

(Pause.)

I can't get the police if you won't. Please Alec.

ALEC: You can if you want.

LISA: Anyone in their right mind would get the police.

ALEC: All right but don't ask me to do it for you.

LISA: I don't like the way you're stopping me.

ALEC: I'm not stopping you.

LISA: I can't do it if when they come in you're just going to sit there.

ALEC: If you want police go and get some. If you don't let's forget it.

LISA: Any other man would get the police himself. He wouldn't put it all on me. You never worry about nothing.

ALEC: So why do you?

LISA: Someone's got to worry to get things done.

ALEC: What really has to be done can just be done. You worry before and you worry afterwards. Most things needn't be done at all.

LISA: Yes, I've noticed. Like work. I often wonder what you're doing all day while I'm washing hair. The boys are kept busy at school. Your mum was busy when she could be.

ALEC: Sitting here quietly. Doing nothing. The day goes by itself.

LISA: I wish you'd see a different doctor who'd find something really wrong with you. Then I could hope you'd get better. I forget normal people are like me. Why can't we try and get our things back?

ALEC: Yes, you must leave me if you want to.

LISA: I always hate it when you say that because what you mean is you want to leave me.

ALEC: No, if I wanted to I would.

LISA: Yes, you would, wouldn't you. You wouldn't worry about

us at all. You wouldn't wonder how I'd bring up the kids.
I can't go on working with a little baby you know. You'd go
away and forget all about us.

ALEC: But I'm not forgetting. I don't want to leave. Here I am.

LISA: Plenty of men do leave their wives but at least they feel
guilty about it.

ALEC: Why not sit down? You must be tired out, you look
awful.

LISA (sitting down): Angie says, you're not still working,
Lisa, not after six months.

(Pause.)

ALEC: It's better you know without that clock ticking. Nothing's
moving at all.

LISA: The baby is.

(ALEC puts his hand out to feel it. Downstairs the front
door shuts. Footsteps come upstairs.)

LISA: I shall scream.

ALEC: If you want to.

(Footsteps. Knock at the door.)

It's not locked.

(WORSELY comes in.)

WORSELY: I hope I'm not intruding. Mrs Crow said she was
sure you wouldn't mind if I had a look round.

LISA: A look round what?

WORSELY: My name is Worsely. Mrs Crow may have
mentioned me. I am a prospective buyer of the house.

LISA: She never said nothing to me.

WORSELY: I think she told you she was intending to sell.

LISA: She said she was thinking about it. That was only a
couple of days ago.

WORSELY: She went to see an estate agent yesterday and the
house is on their new list out today.

LISA: I didn't think she was certain in her mind.

WORSELY: I think she is now.

LISA: It's a bit late at night isn't it for buying a house?

WORSELY: When I viewed the rest of the property this morning there was no reply to my knock. Mrs Crow kindly lent me a spare key because she goes to bed –

LISA: You've got a liberty. What do you want to come frightening people for?

WORSELY: I'm nervous myself. Why am I frightening?

LISA: Have a look round by all means, have a good look round, and you'll see every single thing we own tipped out on the floor. What you don't see is what they took which is what was worth something.

WORSELY: A burglary? I didn't like to wonder. I thought perhaps some matrimonial...are the police making enquiries?

LISA: We haven't told them yet. We've just come in.

WORSELY: Just now? You must be in a state of shock. Can I make some tea? Or wrap you in a blanket? We must get the police at once. What a nuisance there's no telephone in the house.

LISA: No, I'm sorry.

WORSELY: You must be about to rush out to the callbox on the corner. Don't let me detain you. I'll just make myself at home.

LISA: That's all right.

WORSELY: My business can wait.

LISA: We thought we'd leave the police till the morning.

WORSELY: The sooner you go –

LISA: Thank you ever so much. I'm sorry. We're leaving it.

WORSELY: Don't let me interfere of course.

LISA: Do look round at anything you like. The cooker and sink's out on the landing. I expect you saw. I'll clear this lot up. I hardly like to touch my own things. They feel...

WORSELY: Sullied. You could put them all in the drycleaning machine.

LISA: It seems a bit extravagant.

WORSELY: It's what I'd do myself.

LISA: This lot can go to the launderette.

WORSELY: You hear of cases where intruders relieve themselves on the furnishings.

LISA: I don't think I could go on living in a room where that had happened.

WORSELY: I hope you didn't lose anything of great value.

LISA: My engagement ring. That's the worst. And a quite new transistor radio –

WORSELY: And then there's the sentimental value.

LISA: Well there is. I was just saying to Alec.

(They look at him but he doesn't respond. He is lying on the bed by now and stays there for the rest of the scene.)

I don't know what you want to see or I'd show you. It's not a very good room I'm afraid. There's a lot of damp up in that corner. It gets in through the roof. It don't look bad now but it comes up worse in the winter.

WORSELY: I'll have a surveyor of course to see what repairs are necessary.

LISA: It will be nice if you can fix the damp because it's only going to get worse if it's left and it worries me for the winter with the baby.

WORSELY: The back room?

LISA: Yes, would you mind being very quiet because the kids are asleep in there, and Alec's mother. I'm sorry.

WORSELY: I won't go in. I wouldn't dream of it.

LISA: Please do.

WORSELY: I didn't come to wake up your children. That wouldn't be a very good start to our relationship. It's like the room below.

LISA: I've never been in Mrs Crow's rooms. We painted it yellow last year. I don't know if you care for yellow.

WORSELY: Two boys, I think Mrs Crow said. And your mother-in-law?

LISA: Of course when we came it was just my husband and myself. We used to hope we might get a house.

WORSELY: And soon there will be six of you.

LISA: Of course nobody with a decent place would want us in it. I wouldn't myself if I was letting rooms. I'd have single English steady office workers, one in each room. People like you.

WORSELY: Very true.

LISA: So we manage all right.

WORSELY: I expect when Mrs Crow sells the house you'll want to leave.

LISA: I hadn't thought of it.

WORSELY: I thought as you've been friends all these years you might not feel so comfortable when she's gone.

LISA: We're not what you'd call friends.

WORSELY: Especially as you're so overcrowded here.

LISA: Not that we're on bad terms at all.

WORSELY: I'm sure you'd be happier somewhere else.

LISA: Are you turning us out? Is that what you're saying? You can't do that. Alec? We're not furnished you know like the basement.

WORSELY: Turning you out? What an old-fashioned idea. I was hoping I could do you a favour.

LISA: Because this is an unfurnished tenancy.

WORSELY: Moving house is always an expense. You'll want new things for the baby. And then there's your losses tonight. What would you say to two hundred pounds?

LISA: We haven't got two hundred pounds. What do you mean?

WORSELY: No, I'm going to give you two hundred pounds.

LISA: What for?

WORSELY: I was going to say one hundred but seeing I've come at such a catastrophic moment, which I really do sympathize with, I can see my way to making it double.

LISA: How do you mean?

WORSELY: To assist with the removal expenses. To enable you to afford a bigger place. A ground floor perhaps and use of the garden for the kiddies.

LISA: You want to give us two hundred pounds? For nothing?

WORSELY: It's a bit like winning the pools. In a small way.

LISA: Two hundred pound notes?

WORSELY: I like to see people happy.

LISA: You're very kind. Are you sure you can spare it?
You're not just sorry for us are you? You've caught us at
a bad time.

WORSELY: The delightful thing is we both get something out
of it. I get the rooms, you get the money, we're both
happy.

LISA: But they're not our rooms to sell, they're Mrs Crow's.
Shouldn't she have the money? I'm getting all in a muddle,
I'm sorry, but I'm not used to property at all.

WORSELY: Mrs Crow is getting a good price for the house
and this is a little bit extra for you because I like to do
things properly.

LISA: Is this what usually happens?

WORSELY: Very often.

LISA: It's all new to me. Well what an excitement.

ALEC: I'm not moving.

WORSELY: Did your husband say something?

LISA: Have you been paying attention, Alec? Mr Worsely's
giving us two hundred pounds. We mustn't feel bad about
taking it because we'll have the trouble of moving and
he'll have the rooms.

ALEC: We'll have the trouble and he'll have the rooms.

LISA: We can use the money to pay for a bigger place.

ALEC: How much did you say?

LISA: Two hundred pounds.

WORSELY: Two hundred pounds is a lot of money.

LISA: Of course the rents round here have shot up. We'll be
lucky to find something even this size for less than ten.
We only pay two pounds here because it goes back a long
time.

WORSELY: But your new flat would be of a higher standard.

LISA: That's eight into two hundred... It's less than six
months. Is that right? Then we'd have to find all that
extra. Don't think I'm being ungrateful.

WORSELY: You're taking a very unrealistic attitude. I'm only trying to be of assistance.

LISA: I wish it could work out. It seems such a shame.

WORSELY: These conditions are most unsuitable for bringing up a young family. (To ALEC.) All these stairs for your wife. (To LISA.) Three kiddies and their grandmother in one small room.

LISA: What I'd really like is somewhere of my own. I never thought we'd still be here. I saw my life quite different.

WORSELY: You may never have another chance of making a new start. If you try to stay here I think you'll regret it.

LISA: But we don't have to go whatever you say.

WORSELY: Under the new act your rent here will of course be adjusted to a fair rent.

LISA: How much is that?

WORSELY: The property will be so much improved that the rent to be fair – well, we'd have to wait and see, wouldn't we. The builders may find it necessary to take out the stairs for a time. The roof of course will have to come off.

LISA: The roof come off?

WORSELY: You mustn't let that worry you because I'm quite sure that before that happens you'll be snugly installed in some new accomodation. Only don't leave your decision too late because I can't keep my offer open indefinitely.

LISA: It's still open now?

WORSELY: Oh yes, still open for the time being. Suppose I give you a few days and call back one evening next week and we can finalize our arrangements to the greatest benefit of all parties. I wish you luck in getting back your property. You'll need luck as well as the police. I can find my own way down.

(WORSELY goes.)

LISA: We'll never have two hundred pounds all at once to hold in our hands. But it wouldn't last long. I don't know.

ALEC: The best thing is just ignore him.

LISA: We can't ignore him if he walks in. And what did he mean about taking the stairs away and the roof?

ALEC: He wants us to go.

LISA: If he really wants us to go he might offer us even more money. Then we'd have to take it. In our own interests.

ALEC: We don't have to do anything.

LISA: I don't want to stay where I'm not wanted. It's not like home any more. And all our things... Are we getting the police or not?

(Pause.)

Still I've always got the boys, that's what matters. I've got you.

SCENE THREE

Music. MARION, WORSELY, and CLEGG are at a table in a strip club. They have all been drinking, CLEGG most. CLEGG is watching the stripper, the others not.

MARION: I will not sell leasehold. I'll have the freehold first.

WORSELY: You'll have to wait.

MARION: Then I'll wait. And the buyers will wait. The price can only rise.

WORSELY: Arlington understood you would sell.

MARION: I understood I could buy the freehold.

WORSELY: He's expecting –

MARION: But you'll tell him he made a mistake. You're wonderful, Worsely, at anything unpleasant. It's what you're for. Interest him in another property. Forty-two.

WORSELY: We haven't got vacant possession of forty-two.

MARION: But you're working on it, so we soon will. Enjoying yourself Clegg?

CLEGG: Aren't you watching?

MARION: Half.

CLEGG: You're not really entering into it. Doesn't the gun do something for you, Worsely?

WORSELY: It would in my own hands.

CLEGG: She would in my own hands.

MARION: If you want a girl, Clegg, I'll buy you one.

CLEGG: She's never bought me a drink until tonight. Pride.
I have my pride. Tonight's a special occasion. A fling.
The end of Clegg and Son. The end of me.

MARION: Have you been to forty-two?

WORSELY: Three times.

MARION: The basement's no trouble.

WORSELY: The basement's furnished.

MARION: Upstairs. A couple I think with children. And an old
lady.

WORSELY: That's the ones.

CLEGG: Oh now look, did you see that, Marion? Keep a sharp
eye out, Worsely and you won't miss it.

MARION (to WORSELY): How do they seem?

CLEGG: How's that for flesh?

WORSELY (to MARION): Dicey.

MARION (to WORSELY): How far have you gone?

CLEGG: Ooh.

WORSELY (to MARION): Five hundred.

CLEGG: Ooh. Ah.

MARION (to WORSELY): No luck?

WORSELY (to MARION): I could manage the wife.

MARION (to WORSELY): The man?

CLEGG: Ah. Ah.

(Climax. The gun fires. CLEGG gasps. WORSELY jumps
and spills the wine.)

WORSELY: I hate bangs. I'm so sorry. I do apologize.

MARION: I was throwing the dress away in any case. I hate
old clothes. I love to throw them away. And get new ones.

WORSELY: That doesn't look old.

MARION: Old enough.

WORSELY: You don't look old.

MARION: I should hope not. You're no good at flattery,
Worsely, but luckily I'm too vain to mind.

CLEGG: Wasn't that... quite... interesting really? Worth every penny.

MARION: I believe I know the tenants at forty-two.

WORSELY: Minton.

MARION: Lisa Minton. She does hair. And... Alec?

CLEGG: What?

MARION: Fancy them being my tenants.

WORSELY: Friends are they?

CLEGG: What?

MARION: Do you remember Lisa and Alec, Clegg?

CLEGG: What do you mean, do I remember?

MARION: Do you remember?

CLEGG: You sound as if I might have forgotten.

MARION: It's some time.

CLEGG: It is indeed.

WORSELY: Old friends?

CLEGG: Friends of Marion's.

MARION: You liked Lisa.

CLEGG: I liked Lisa.

WORSELY: You found him a bit odd, I expect.

CLEGG: Marion got on with him all right.

(Music starts again.)

MARION: It's a long time ago.

CLEGG: Why have they come up?

WORSELY: Marion's bought the house they live in.

CLEGG: What for?

MARION: To sell. Look, it's starting again and none of us watching. What a waste.

CLEGG: Worsely deals with it does he?

WORSELY: I call from time to time. They're trying it on.

CLEGG: I'm sure Worsely will deal with it very well Marion. You won't need to go round yourself.

MARION: I trust Worsely to do everything I would do.

CLEGG: Let him do it then.

MARION: Do look, Clegg. I do think these girls are so clever. I would never dare. Would I? I don't think so.

CLEGG: You? Dare? You'd better not, Marion. It's all right for them, it's what they do. We pay for it. You haven't got the figure in any case, so remember your place. Loose talk costs lives.

MARION: What if I did it for you?

CLEGG: For me? Would you? Like that. Look, Worsely, you're missing the best – look at that, Marion. Remember that. Ah, that was close.

WORSELY: You know them then?

MARION: Some time ago. We lost touch.

WORSELY: You remember them quite well.

MARION: Lisa phoned me this morning. She said was it right I knew about property these days because she was in some trouble and needed advice.

CLEGG: Oh Marion look at the size of them... oh I'd like to get hold. Oh I'd like to gobble...

MARION: I said she could call at the office on Wednesday morning. So you might keep clear for a start.

WORSELY: Be careful.

CLEGG: Oh stop it. Ooh.

MARION: I always am.

WORSELY: I know.

CLEGG: Ooh. Aah. Oh my goodness gracious. Ooh.

MARION: He's busy.

WORSELY: Careful.

MARION: Do as you're told.

(They kiss. CLEGG is intent on the strip.)

SCENE FOUR

MARION'S office. Large desk and large street map. MARION
and LISA. MARION is on her feet, eating a bar of chocolate.
LISA is sitting in a chair on the client's side of the desk,
huge and tired.

LISA: Mrs Crow keeps saying, Nobody wants a property with
tenants. As if it was rats. Why don't they put poison down?
She says, If you're an owner, dear, you expect to own.
Why don't you save up and get your own place like I did.
She got that house before the war for two hundred pounds
and now it's twenty thousand. I wasn't born when I could
have got it for two hundred. So I don't care if that Worsely
won't like the noise. I'll tell the kids they can shout all
they want and get up at six and jump off the bed onto the
floor. One thing if we don't have stairs I won't hear him
coming up them. My blood runs cold. He comes at night
just to make it worse. He takes a look all round the room
to see how he's going to improve it. He'll get rid of the
old wallpaper, he'll get rid of the damp, he'll get rid of us.

MARION: Five hundred pounds is a good offer.

LISA: If it was just me I'd go.

MARION: Not enough?

LISA: He don't seem to notice Worsely at all. You know what
he's like.

MARION: Not really.

LISA: You don't, do you. Not now. You'd see a change. He's
very queer. Oh Marion he is. The past is over isn't it
Marion? I wouldn't have come to you for help if I hadn't
thought all that was such a long time ago. But we all had
some good times once. I don't know who else I could ask
that knows about houses. And really I'd rather have him
unfaithful than like what he is now. It's half what you
expect from a man. My mum always said not to take on
and they'd soon be back. And it's quite true, nothing ever
lasted. Because men know in their hearts where they
belong. But she never said nothing about someone being
like Alec is now. He hasn't been at work for six months.
He don't remember to eat if I don't make him. He's very
nice to me all the time. But I sometimes wonder if he
knows who I am. I think he'd be nice to anyone. I went to
see the doctor about him and he gave me some pills to take
myself but that don't make Alec any better it just makes

me put up with it. And now they've stopped cheering me
up anyway. And I'm worried, Marion, they might have hurt
the baby. I don't think Alec would care if it was a good
pretty baby or a monster. I don't think he could tell the
difference.

MARION: What does he do? What does he talk about?

LISA: Nothing at all. He don't get bored. He was always
rushing about wasn't he? Marion, I'm really frightened
by him. I can't start looking for a place with him like that.
If I have to do one more thing I'll scream. When I think of
the nights and nappies I hope this baby's never born.

MARION: Alec was never stubborn. He always rather gave
in to what you wanted.

LISA: If I insisted he might give in. But I don't know what I
want any more. And in a funny way he does. He just wants
nothing. He seems to feel everything's all right.

MARION: He stays in all day? And in the evening?

LISA: It's not like it was. There's nobody else. It's almost
like a very happy time. If things was different. He's lovely
with the boys when he bothers.

MARION: Does Alec want the baby?

(Knock at the door. MARION opens it. It is WORSELY.
LISA doesn't look round.)

No, not now. Five minutes. Go away.

(She shuts the door.)

Now, Lisa, what are you going to do?

LISA: I don't know. I came to ask you. Since you know about
property. You don't know of somewhere we could go?

MARION: Not at the rent you're paying now of course.

LISA: Mr Worsely says it's going up. He won't say what to.
So you might as well go, he says. But go where?

MARION: Would Alec go if I found you another flat?

LISA: Perhaps if you could come and talk to him. You could
tell him it's what you recommend as an expert.

MARION: If you really think that would help.

LISA: I tell myself Mr Worsely's just saying things to frighten
me but he does frighten me. I wouldn't ask you if I wasn't

desperate. I didn't want to see you again. But I can't have a baby with the roof off.

(Knock at the door.)

MARION (answering the door): I said – oh it's you. What's the matter?

(CLEGG comes in.)

CLEGG: I just thought I'd drop in. I got a bit bored indoors. Sambo's excellent company for a dog. He does just what he's told as if he was human. I pretended to be cross, just to see, and he lay down with eyes so sad just like a real member of the family, and then I said, Good fellow, come –

MARION: Lisa.

CLEGG: And he leapt – well well. Expecting again. Congratulations.

LISA: We was always such friends.

CLEGG: It's a long time. Things were very different. You've heard our tragedy I suppose? I've had to close the shop.

LISA: Oh no, you've never had to do that. What an awful thing. Your very own shop all gone.

CLEGG: That's what I say. All gone. My very own.

LISA: You're as badly off as me.

CLEGG: It's a man's job to put a stiff upper lip on the face of it. To lend a supporting arm. Your chin can tremble.

LISA: It's such a relief to feel I'm with real old friends.

CLEGG: Sympathy may not do any good but it does help.

LISA: Oh it does. I'm so glad. Oh forgive me. (Cries.)

CLEGG: There there. A real woman. A good cry. Best thing.

MARION: Can we get on?

LISA: I'm so tired of it all.

CLEGG: There there there.

LISA: Oh oh.

CLEGG: Poor little flower.

LISA: Oh.

(Knock. MARION opens the door. It is WORSELY. MARION

is about to stop him, then gives up.)

MARION: Oh what the hell.

(WORSELY comes in.)

CLEGG (to WORSELY): A moving moment.

MARION: Come over here where we can hear ourselves think. Has Arlington seen forty-two yet?

WORSELY: He'd like it with vacant possession. Is that her?

MARION: You're very white.

WORSELY: It's the gas.

MARION: What, last night?

WORSELY: That Samaritan friend of mine dropped in just as I was going off nicely.

MARION: Had you invited him?

WORSELY: You know me better than that Marion. I do try.

LISA: Mr Worsely?

WORSELY: At your service as always. I hope you've come to a happy decision.

LISA: You know him?

CLEGG: He's Marion's employee my dear. He goes about to all her properties dealing with the tenants. Have a hanky. Blow.

LISA: You mean it's you buying the house? It's all you, Marion, is it? I always hated you, you horrible bitch, you cunt cunt cunt –

CLEGG: I hate to hear a lady use language.

MARION: Have a cry. Have a good cry. Then we'll see.

SCENE FIVE

Room. ALEC is on the bed and his MUM is in the armchair asleep. From time to time she slips down and has to be propped up. MARION is standing, eating a banana taken from a bowl on the table. She gives him an orange, which he takes but doesn't eat.

MARION: I'm always hungry. But thin. I don't put on. Nothing to show for it. Moving about all the time is what does it.

I eat in bed. I work at the table and sleep at my desk. Burning it up.

ALEC: Help yourself.

MARION: I do. Is something wrong with your legs?

ALEC: No.

MARION: Or your head?

ALEC: No.

MARION: Why don't you get up?

ALEC: If you like.

(He gets up.)

MARION: Alec you know it's me that's bought the house.

ALEC: Lisa told me.

MARION: Worsely acts for me.

ALEC: She said.

MARION: I want vacant possession of my house.

ALEC: I gather.

MARION: Lisa suggested I came and talked to you. I can offer alternative accomodation. I wouldn't have come otherwise.

ALEC: No.

MARION: I would have come anyway.

ALEC: Yes.

MARION: I knew you were here when I bought the house. That was why. Also the property itself. Desirable investment. How could I have bought it without knowing unless I'd forgotten the address and I couldn't do that. I've a great memory for details. All sorts of little details.

ALEC: Marion, what do you want?

MARION: I'll give you a thousand pounds to go away.

ALEC: I don't want a thousand pounds.

MARION: What do you want?

ALEC: Nothing at all. I try to want things for Lisa. For the boys. For mum even though she's past wanting anything she can have. I don't know what I could lose that would make any difference to me.

MARION: Lisa?

ALEC: No.

MARION: You don't love her.

ALEC: I didn't say that.

MARION: If you love someone you want to keep them. I want
to. So not Lisa. Your mum? Lisa says you won't part with
her. You won't let her go to hospital. Do you cling to your
mum?

ALEC: She'll die soon.

MARION: Are you sorry?

ALEC: Everyone dies. Unless they were never born.

MARION: Are you glad then?

ALEC: No.

MARION: Have you got no feelings at all?

ALEC: Not of indignation.

MARION: But you wouldn't want to lose your children.

ALEC: No.

MARION: There then.

ALEC: But children do die sometimes. It could happen. Why
not to mine as much as someone else's?

MARION: But if it did happen to yours, that should be a horror
for you. We're not talking about other people.

ALEC: I could probably bear it.

MARION: I'll give you a thousand pounds for Lisa. For your
mum. For the boys. Whatever you like to think it's for.
And find you somewhere to live. This flat is ridiculous.

ALEC: You seem to want this house very much.

MARION: What I want is you to wake up. We were going to
better ourselves. What did we go to evening classes for?
We both felt we'd missed something. You were never sure
what subject was the answer. Everything seemed to lead
to something else you wanted to get hold of. There were
books in the bed. You couldn't let a single fact go.

ALEC: Learning things wasn't any use.

MARION: If you wanted it to be some use you should have

concentrated on one thing and got a qualification. I got on in the end in my own way. I always said I wasn't the butcher's wife. You could have done something even greater.

ALEC: But why should I?

MARION: You've no stamina. (Pause.) I've got a garden flat you could have.

ALEC: Basement.

MARION: Basement flat.

ALEC: Do you want us to go really?

MARION: Two thousand pounds to get out of my house.

ALEC: Why do you think I want two thousand pounds?

MARION: You should want it. For Lisa's sake. For your sons. What are you up to, Alec? Of course it wasn't in your interest to go for two hundred or five hundred or whatever little sum it was. Even a thousand doesn't touch the profit I'll make. I respect you for hanging on. But two thousand? Two five.

MUM: Edie. Edie.

ALEC: Hello there.

MARION: Are you Edie?

ALEC: She likes someone to answer.

(He goes over to MUM and props her up.)

MARION: My God, I hope I don't live as long.

ALEC: She's not in pain.

MARION: Marvellous.

ALEC: It's a great deal.

MARION: But she doesn't know what's going on. Does she remember her own life? Does she even know who she is? I'd kill myself if I felt my mind beginning to drop away like that. Suppose I said, Alec, Alec, and someone else said Hello there. And I didn't know it wasn't you. Because it would be you I called for even if I was eighty.

ALEC: I've always thought of that as over. In fact I never think of it at all.

MARION: My face will go like hers one day. I keep what I can.

I don't want to die.

ALEC: It was all here before you were born and you don't resent that.

MARION: But once you have things you don't want to give them up. It's quite different.

ALEC: No, it's just the same.

MARION: But I want to hold on. Everything I was taught – be clean, be quick, be top, be best, you may not succeed, Marion, but what matters is to try your hardest. To push on. Onward Christian soldiers, marching as to war. That was my favourite song when I was seven. Fight the good fight. Where's your fight? I know the bible stories aren't true but that makes their meaning matter most. God gave him dominion over every beast of the field and fowl of the air. Gave the land to him and to his seed forever. Doesn't evolution say the same? Keep on, get better, be best. Onward. Fight. How did man get to the moon? Not by sitting staring at an orange. Columbus, Leonardo de Vinci, Scott of the Antarctic. You would be content on a flat earth. But the animals are ours. The vegetables and minerals. For us to consume. We don't shrink from blood. Or guilt. Guilt is essential to progress. You'll tell me next you don't feel guilt. I don't know how you know you're alive. Guilt is knowing what you do. I see the children with no shoes and socks in the houses I buy. Should I buy them socks? It would be ridiculous. But I feel it. That gritty lump is the pearl. Swine. And what would happen to work without guilt? I was never a lazy girl, Marion tries hard. I work like a dog. Most women are fleas but I'm the dog.

ALEC: I don't at all mind leaving if you want it very much.

MARION: Two five?

ALEC: No money.

MARION: Lisa will want it.

ALEC: All right, if you like. If she likes. Talk about it to her.

MUM: Edie.

ALEC: Hello. (He goes across to sit her up.)

MARION: Wouldn't you rather stay here?

ALEC: I don't mind.

MARION: You could stay.

ALEC: Of course I could.

MARION: I mean there would be no more pressure.

ALEC: Yes Lisa doesn't like Worsely much.

MARION: No more Worsely.

ALEC: Good.

MARION: Are you with me?

ALEC: I don't think so, no.

MARION: You could stay here as long as you like. If we could go back.

ALEC: Back where?

MARION: To each other.

ALEC: I wasn't at all the same person then.

MARION: You were mine then and you always will be.

ALEC: I've changed. Skin and all in seven years.

MARION: The mind's the same. Don't wriggle, Alec.

ALEC: I don't know what mind you mean.

MARION: You can say what you like but it's still recognizably you. Of course you're not exactly the same. Everyone changes. But this you is in place of that you. It's still you. It's not someone else altogether.

ALEC: I think it might just as well be. You talk about the past and the future but it doesn't apply. Here I am now.

MARION: What you're saying is you've had a breakdown.

ALEC: Or up. Or through.

MARION: I've been in a mental hospital myself. Just after.

ALEC: I heard.

MARION: I don't care if you're mad or sane, Alec. I'm yours whether you want me or not. Have all the money and stay here too if that's what you want. Empires have been lost for love. Worlds well lost. We men of destiny get what we're after even if we're destroyed by it. And everyone else with us. We split the atom. Onward. Love me.

ALEC: I'm not what you want.

MARION: You are what I want. I want you badly now.

ALEC: Now?

MARION: And always. I'm keeping you Alec.

ALEC: I could now. Easily. If you want. But I don't keep.

MUM: Edie. Edie.

SCENE SIX

Same. Old MUM has slipped well down in her chair and almost fallen out. LISA is lying on the bed. She has come in from work. ALEC is standing near. MARION is eating.

LISA: Might have known.

ALEC: It wasn't planned.

MARION: Speak for yourself.

LISA: I wouldn't have come in early if this hadn't started. I might never have known.

MARION: Yes it was bad luck.

LISA: It was not. I like to know. So I can forgive him. Or not. Whichever I want to do.

MARION: You were just in time if you want to know. If you're technically minded.

LISA: I don't need to know the details. Here's another.

MARION: You're meant to relax I've heard. You won't do that with me here.

ALEC: Shall I get the ambulance yet?

LISA: Don't you dare. I'm not lying round in hospital a minute longer than I need to. Alec, you'll have to do the boys tea.

ALEC: Don't worry.

LISA: Tell them where I've gone.

ALEC: Don't worry.

MARION: You can stay here, Lisa, by the way. I lose quite a few thousand pounds. I must ask Mr Arlington if he's pre- pared to buy the house with sitting tenants. And if not find him another house. And this house another purchaser. So don't mention all your thanks.

LISA: I'm not staying here. With you two.

MARION: If you go you don't get any money.

LISA: I'll see you in hell. Hold my hand Alec.

ALEC: You're lovely.

MARION (propping up old MUM): Up she comes.

LISA: It's three weeks early.

ALEC: Don't worry.

LISA: I'm not bringing a baby home to this. I am not. I'd sooner kill it.

MARION: You were quite happy to stay here before. You refused our offers of financial assistance with the move.

LISA: I was never happy.

MARION: You mean you want to go? All right, go. I'll be only too glad.

LISA: I don't know.

MARION: Stay then. Are you staying?

LISA: You can have it. If you think it's so easy.

MARION: I don't want it to live in.

LISA: You can have the baby.

MARION: What does she mean? Having a baby you have to do yourself.

LISA: Afterwards. You have it. I'm not.

MARION: Have the baby?

LISA: I'm not bringing a baby back to this room.

MARION: I'll take it, yes.

LISA: You take it then. I never want to see it.

MARION: I'll take it then. I'll keep it.

LISA: Yes keep it.

ALEC: I'm getting the ambulance, Lisa.

LISA: Both of you go.

MARION: I could stay with you if I have to. Though I wouldn't know what to do.

LISA: Alec, don't leave me alone with her.

ALEC: All right?

(ALEC and MARION go out. OLD MUM slips right down, starts, wakes.)

MUM: Edie? Edie. Make you cuppa tea.

(She gets up and walks across the room. She goes out onto the landing. She comes back in with the kettle and puts it on the table. She walks slowly around looking for the tea. She finds the teapot and takes it to the table. She finds the matches and puts them on the table. Dizzy for a moment, she holds onto the table. She pours water from the kettle to the teapot, spilling most of it over the matches. She sits trying to strike the matches. LISA is lying on the bed. Once her face creases and she breathes deeply as she has a contraction - no exaggerated moaning or writhing about. Then she lies limp as before.)

Act Two

CLEGG and WORSELY in Clegg's kitchen. Large pram.
CLEGG is heating a baby's bottle in a saucepan of water.
WORSELY is making tea. His neck is bandaged.

CLEGG: Weedkiller.

WORSELY: Sugar.

CLEGG: Two for me.

WORSELY: I wouldn't try to hang myself again.

CLEGG: Weedkiller in Marion's soup. In a garlic soup. Would
it taste?

WORSELY: Try some and see.

CLEGG: I read of someone got just a splash in an orange drink
and poured it away when she tasted but even so that sip was
fatal. It took a week mind you.

WORSELY: You'd have a job explaining.

CLEGG: I don't care. I don't care. I've had enough bottling
up. Something must explode.

WORSELY: My befriender the Samaritan believes life is God-
given. At first he was too sensitive to say so but now in
the interests of our befriendship he talks about his real
feelings. Life is leasehold. It belongs to God the almighty
landlord. You mustn't take your life because it's God's
property not yours. I tell him if there's anything I own it's
what I stand up in.

CLEGG: That old suit?

WORSELY: My flesh and blood. The contraption I am in. The
contraption I am.

CLEGG: It's not illegal now I'm glad to say. I couldn't have
let Marion employ a criminal.

WORSELY: Why was it illegal? The life as property of the
state?

CLEGG: In the free world?

WORSELY: In wartime it is.

CLEGG: In wartime, naturally. No, I believe it was against the law because it was wrong morally.

WORSELY: And now it no longer is?

CLEGG: Apparently not.

WORSELY: Though in any case the law's not for morals so much as property. The legal system was made by owners. A man can do what he likes with his own.

CLEGG: Try telling Marion.

WORSELY: A house the same. Your own. You knock the floor out if you like. That's what it's for. A car the same. You drive how you like. Within a reasonable speed limit. My flesh and blood the same.

CLEGG: A wife the same.

WORSELY: A wife is a person.

CLEGG: First and foremost a wife. One flesh. Marion leaves me.

WORSELY: She's basically fond.

CLEGG: Every morning she leaves me to go to work.

WORSELY: Work's a virtue.

CLEGG: And every evening she leaves me, leaves me, leaves me.

WORSELY: Goes out?

CLEGG: Or stays in. But not with me. Not being my wife. Not paying attention.

WORSELY: She's a lot on her mind.

CLEGG: Like what?

WORSELY: The baby?

CLEGG: And?

WORSELY: Business?

CLEGG: And?

WORSELY: I'm not specially close to Marion to know her thoughts.

CLEGG: Not close?

WORSELY: No.

CLEGG: These days.

WORSELY: Pardon?

CLEGG: Not so close as you were?

WORSELY: She's a bit absent-minded as you say.

CLEGG: I will chop her mind into little pieces and blanch them in boiling water.

WORSELY: Baby's looking well.

CLEGG: You are looking, Worsely, at a man who has killed a man.

WORSELY: Pardon me?

CLEGG: More than you have done. Manhood, Worsely. Some of us may think we have it when really it is someone else.

WORSELY: How do you mean?

CLEGG: I changed a living human being into a carcass.

WORSELY: Who was it?

CLEGG: I don't know who it was, that's not the point, who it was. It was me did it, that's the point. 'Who was it'!

WORSELY: When was it then?

CLEGG: Twenty years ago.

WORSELY: I was only a toddler.

CLEGG: I was a man.

WORSELY: Before my time. I'm not an accessory?

CLEGG: Man to man.

WORSELY: Some time back. No repercussions?

CLEGG: How do you mean?

WORSELY: Of course most murders do go undetected. The police don't publicize the fact.

CLEGG: It wasn't a murder.

WORSELY: You mean we're talking about an accident? I ran over a little boy with my motor scooter when I was seventeen, I don't make a song and dance.

CLEGG: It was in the army. National Service we men had to

do.

WORSELY: Oh the army. Why didn't you say so? Anyone can kill somebody if they're in the army. Was it one of the enemy?

CLEGG: It was a guerilla.

WORSELY: You were claiming just now it was a man.

CLEGG: Guerilla, little chappies in the bushes.

WORSELY: Oh, I thought you meant – never mind.

CLEGG: It was him or me.

WORSELY: It doesn't count if you were in uniform. Everybody knows it's not the same thing as killing another person.

CLEGG: It does count.

WORSELY: I've a cousin in America reckons he killed any number. But what does he expect in the situation they've got in? I don't think that makes him special.

CLEGG: But did he see them?

WORSELY: He didn't say. It was just a postcard.

CLEGG: I can see it might not be the same if you don't see them. Bombing from a plane.

WORSELY: Bombing's not what I call killing.

CLEGG: Not at all.

WORSELY: You can't feel over a certain distance.

CLEGG: Well in my case at about twenty feet I felt quite a shock.

WORSELY: I dare say you might.

CLEGG: Just so long as you know who it's the wife of you're dealing with.

WORSELY: Bottle's hot.

CLEGG: Blast.

WORSELY: Cool it.

CLEGG: Damn nuisance. Night time too. (He puts the bottle in a bowl of cold water.)

WORSELY: Does he wake you?

CLEGG: You try spending the night here some time.

WORSELY: I wouldn't mind.

CLEGG: Watch your tone of voice.

WORSELY: I mean I quite take to that baby. I always thought they all looked alike. But I'd know him.

CLEGG: How?

WORSELY: Sort of dimple.

CLEGG: Plenty of them about.

WORSELY: It's the general look. I saw a baby yesterday in the street. I looked in the pram and it wasn't him. Same colour pram. Same size baby. But different look.

CLEGG: You give him the bottle. You be dad.

WORSELY: If he gets kidnapped any time and you have to go and identify him you can take me. Marion wouldn't know.

CLEGG: She sleeps like the dead. I kick her. Punch her in the kidneys. No avail.

WORSELY: He's not awake for his bottle.

CLEGG: It's bottle time.

WORSELY: You don't wake him?

CLEGG: He's got to learn regular habits. He won't make a family butcher without a sense of responsibility. Waking in the night's no substitute.

WORSELY: Butcher is he?

CLEGG: Marion thinks she's bought me off. I've a gun upstairs.

(WORSELY was about to pick up the baby but now forgets about it.)

WORSELY: Real one?

CLEGG: Old customer did me a favour. Get all sorts buying meat. No questions asked.

WORSELY: Loaded?

CLEGG: Wait and see.

WORSELY: I couldn't borrow it could I one night? I would have finished with it by tomorrow.

CLEGG: How were you planning to give it back?

WORSELY: I want it.

CLEGG: Of course if I was to think I had any reason to suspect anything of you, Worsely, then I might help you on your way.

WORSELY: Me?

CLEGG: Tell me plainly do you fuck my wife? Or does she jerk you off? Or do you touch her up? Or snog? Fumble? Grope? Caress? Brush against? Or come very close to any of these?

WORSELY: You've got the wrong man.

CLEGG: How close?

WORSELY: Alec.

CLEGG: Proof.

WORSELY: Beyond a reasonable doubt.

CLEGG: Seen?

WORSELY: I wouldn't look.

CLEGG: Said?

WORSELY: Changed, just she's changed.

CLEGG: Changed to you?

WORSELY: All round.

CLEGG: You mean she used to and now she won't.

WORSELY: Anything I can do Clegg as an old friend of the family and employee of your wife I will gladly do to rid us of Alec.

CLEGG: To rid me of Alec.

WORSELY: That's what I said. Don't push me Clegg. It makes my head wobble.

CLEGG: Weedkiller.

WORSELY: Let's have a look.

CLEGG: It says poison in red here.

WORSELY: I know it is. (He takes the packet and keeps it.)

CLEGG: There's the gun. But I was keeping that for her.

WORSELY: I'm jumpy of bangs. Though I could if it was myself because you wouldn't hear, would you, the explosion causing your own extinction?

CLEGG: What I had in mind, Worsely. What I have had in mind for some time. Was a fire.

WORSELY: Like an electric fire dropped in the bath? But I doubt if he uses the Arlingtons' bathroom.

CLEGG: Set the house on fire. Set the house on fire.

WORSELY: Easily said.

CLEGG: Easily done. Petrol and so on.

WORSELY: There are other people.

CLEGG: They would get out. They would probably all get out.

WORSELY: Alec would get out.

CLEGG: Never mind, he might not. It's the idea. The threat to him. The damage to Marion. Her property you see.

WORSELY: Arlington completed last week.

CLEGG: It's somewhat symbolic. Think of the terror.

WORSELY: What do I get out of it?

CLEGG: You could try pouring petrol on yourself.

WORSELY: I think I should be paid.

CLEGG: Fifty pounds? Hundred.

WORSELY: Look, Marion will pay, don't you see? You get the money off Marion. You only have to ask.

CLEGG: What have you got against her, Worsely? I'm prepared to sink any differences in a common cause. Afterwards I'd like you to leave the area. You could set up in property yourself. London is full of property.

WORSELY: Thousand?

CLEGG: Leaving me with my wife and son to bring up as I please.

(WORSELY pours two more mugs of tea.)

WORSELY: I think I'll just pop out and kill some weeds. Very weedy garden.

CLEGG: A baby's a full time job. I'm not a gardener.

WORSELY: So I'll do a bit for you. All right?

(He sets off out of the back door with weedkiller, mug of tea, packet of sugar.)

CLEGG: Don't take all the sugar. What about me. I take two.

(WORSELY has gone. CLEGG feels the temperature of the bottle: too cold. He mutters and puts it back in the saucepan to warm up. Loud explosion. CLEGG opens the back door.)

Christ, Worsely, you've blown off your hand.

SCENE TWO

Marion's office. MARION and LISA. MARION is walking about eating. LISA, no longer pregnant, hair a mess, face a wreck, baggy old dress, is sitting in a chair, crying.

LISA: I can't stop crying.

MARION: What about?

LISA: I don't know.

MARION: Then it doesn't matter. So long as you're not sad about anything. I should just cry.

LISA: It's the pills they give me.

MARION: There's plenty of tissues.

LISA: You never cry.

MARION: Not over nothing, no.

LISA: I'm getting worse and worse. I want to get better, Marion.

MARION: Home soon.

LISA: Marion I want...

MARION: Tissue.

LISA: No no. I want...

MARION: Get on with it.

LISA: To see him.

MARION: Who?

LISA: My baby.

MARION: He's not here.

LISA: I want to see him.

MARION: No you don't.

LISA: I want to.

MARION: It's not supposed to be good. You're not even meant to see me. Just the third party. That's Worsely but he's late.

LISA: Why not?

MARION: In a third party adoption, Lisa, each party sees the third party and all emotion is thus kept out.

LISA: I want him.

MARION: You want to get better, Lisa, and look after your boys. Alec's taken his mother to hospital. Right? So you've got to look after your big boys. That's your duty, Lisa, to your family.

LISA: I can't stop crying.

MARION: Cry then for God's sake. Nobody's stopping you.

LISA: I may not earn so much money as you. But I'm not worth nothing.

MARION: Nobody said you were not worth nothing.

LISA: I'm sorry Marion, it's the pills. There's nothing wrong with me.

(WORSELY comes in. His right arm is heavily bandaged.)

MARION: Late.

WORSELY: Mr Nicolaides barred my way with a poker.

MARION: Haven't they gone?

WORSELY: The wife died of cancer.

MARION: I don't see how that helps. Where are the papers?

WORSELY: Here we are. What's the trouble, Lisa?

MARION: He doesn't expect an answer. You sign here.

LISA: What is it?

MARION: Just a formality.

WORSELY: To make you feel secure in your tenure.

LISA: What?

WORSELY: The flat. You're staying in the flat, Lisa. I won't ever call on you again.

LISA: Is that what it says?

WORSELY: Legal jargon.

LISA: It swims about.

MARION: Terrible small print, I quite agree.

LISA: What does it say?

WORSELY: It just confirms all the arrangements.

LISA: What does it say about the baby?

MARION: Nothing new.

LISA: What? I can't read it.

MARION: No need.

WORSELY: Sign here.

LISA: After can I see the baby?

WORSELY: Don't drip all over the paper.

LISA: I want to see he's all right.

MARION: Of course he is.

LISA: Because later when I'm better I'll have him back.

WORSELY: He's very well taken care of. I wouldn't lie.

(LISA signs the paper.)

LISA: Can I see him now?

MARION: He's at home in his own pram with his own daddy.
Now that's all done. Good. Finished.

LISA: I can't stop crying.

WORSELY: I wish you would Lisa, you make me feel quite
ill. Cheer up. You're the sort of reason I do myself inuries.

LISA: I can't stop. I can't stop. I can't stop.

(MARION slaps her. She stops crying.)

MARION: That's the thing to do. If it was me I'd do the same.

WORSELY: I'll take you home, Lisa, in a taxi.

LISA: You've got so kind again Mr Worsely. Like the first
time you came. You won't suddenly take off the roof?

(LISA goes out. WORSELY turns back at the door.)

WORSELY (to MARION): All right? And I'm going home after.

MARION: You don't have to work for me you know.

WORSELY: I'll tell you when I've stopped.

MARION: She's not fit, you see. And I need it more. I'll make
far better use.

WORSELY: I'll still do almost anything for you. Marion?

MARION: Not yet.

WORSELY: You'll turn to me one day and find me dead.

MARION: I'll take the risk.

WORSELY: The times that are unbearable come closer
together and last longer. What when they all join up?

MARION: Do what you want. Get what you can.

SCENE THREE

Hospital cubicle. Alec's MUM in bed, fixed up to a drip. ALEC
is sitting by the bed. After a moment MARION comes in. She
has brought a bunch of grapes, which she soon starts eating.

MARION: Any change?

ALEC: Not that I've noticed.

MARION: You can't say they don't try.

(Pause.)

There's a girl along there been unconscious six months.
It's marvellous how they can keep you alive once they get
you on those machines. The machine just runs on and
you're part of it. An expensive way of life. And what is it
they're keeping alive? It still looks like a person of course,
which is why they go to all the trouble. If it looked like a
vegetable marrow, which is how it behaves and probably
how it feels, they wouldn't bother.

(Pause.)

Still she might suddenly sit up and then you'd be sorry if
you'd let her die.

(Pause.)

On the other hand, what a life.

(Pause.)

Still a vegetable is a vegetable. You don't smash it up just
for being a vegetable.

(Pause.)

On the other hand there's plenty of other people.

(Pause.)

Still if it was you I expect I'd be glad you were still there. In some sense. I could still recognize it as you.

ALEC: It wouldn't matter.

MARION: What?

ALEC: If it was there or not.

MARION: Not to you. To me it would make all the difference.

ALEC: I don't mind for myself the way you go on but you won't get what you want.

MARION: I was talking about matters of general interest. I do try not to grab at you.

ALEC: Next Monday I'll be back at work.

MARION: What as?

ALEC: A glazier, like I was.

MARION: I thought you stopped because you didn't like it. You're not stretched. You have still got ambition whether you want to or not.

ALEC: It's hard to say really why I stopped.

MARION: You couldn't see a future. I'm sure you have a great career ahead as something you hardly dream of. There's no limit. It's finding where to start. Before I started on property I just had no idea of myself. You don't know what you're capable of till you suddenly find yourself doing it. Does property appeal to you at all?

ALEC: I'd rather not have an idea of myself.

MARION: At least you'll be doing something again. That's a start. Do you feel better now?

ALEC: Nothing special.

MARION: I couldn't go up high on those big buildings. I've no head. I think you're wasting yourself.

ALEC: I knew a man fell fifty feet once and he wasn't hurt. Then on the way home he stepped under a bus.

MARION: But usually if you fall fifty feet you do get hurt.

There's always traffic but falling's extra.

ALEC: Some people take care of themselves and they're all
right. Some people take care and they're not. Some don't
take care and they're all right. Some people don't and
they're not.

MARION: But still there is what's probable.

ALEC: Not certain.

MARION: Insurance companies make money on it.

ALEC: It does work, yes.

(Pause.)

MARION: Do you stay here all day?

ALEC: I'll stay a bit longer anyway.

MARION: Does she know if somebody's here?

ALEC: I don't think she knows anything does she? I shouldn't
think.

(Pause.)

MARION: Some men were playing music in the tube. I heard
it floating up round the corner as I came down the stairs,
and I thought whatever's that, that's nice. I like music,
specially if it's a surprise. I expect they get moved on
though because it's public property. The boy that took my
money smiled right in my eyes, and later when I saw my
reflection in the train window I was smiling and smiling.
I hardly knew it was me. Of course it is a very dark
reflection. But after all what is all that? I don't know him.
He doesn't know me. It could have been anyone. All that
smiling would still have happened.

ALEC: But it was you.

MARION: But he didn't know it was me. Not who I know I am.
Not what I know is important about me. Not my ideas. And
what I've done. And what I've got. Not me.

ALEC: But nor do I.

MARION: You try not to. You try not to know me. I know all
I can about you.

ALEC: Let it go.

MARION: After she's dead, leave Lisa. I'll leave Clegg. You
can choose where we go to. I can pay for anywhere in the

world. Couldn't you do with some sun? Or snow. Snow
might suit you better. We could go somewhere in the arctic
circle where you wouldn't see anyone for weeks. Wherever
you look it's white. You have to wear dark glasses for the
glare. On and on, on sledges, and never anything different
to see. You always did want to travel. You've a restless
nature. You always felt tied by Lisa. I wouldn't tie you.
I don't expect you to believe that. But you can't imagine
how wonderfully I could let you be once I was sure of you.
Just say yes, and we'll be gone. I'll arrange every detail
myself.

ALEC: No.

MARION: But you don't love Lisa more than me. Compare us
and I'm better in every way. She's not so clever. Not so
attractive. To you she's not, not just objectively. She's
not even got a particularly nice nature. Though even not
particularly nice might be nicer than me, but she's not
much of a personality. She doesn't even begin to understand
you. I do begin. She's not your equal and I am. I love
you more than she does. I'd give up more. I've more to
give up. And you know yourself you love me more than her.

ALEC: I don't think I could say I loved anyone more than
anyone else.

MARION: You love me more than a complete stranger.

ALEC: I couldn't say for certain. I can say I love you and
Lisa. But it wouldn't matter if I never saw you again.

MARION: It's no use being loved like that. You love your
children more than someone else's.

ALEC: Not necessarily. You see.

MARION: But you've got to. Everyone loves their own – loves.

ALEC: Slowly everything...fell through. Lisa, children,
work – there was no point. There was no point in the things
I wanted instead. There wasn't any point in killing myself.
That went on for some time. I didn't know how to make
things better. I didn't care if they were better or not. I
didn't know what better meant. But now the same things
seem quite simple. Lisa, children, work, why not?

MARION: If you got bored with them before you'll just get
bored with them again.

ALEC: I longed very much one morning for the sea in winter.

Grey sea, I thought, gritty sand. So I leapt up from the bed, grabbed a train, went. I got there and it was nothing special. Grey sea, like I thought, gritty sand.

MARION: A let down.

ALEC: No, not at all. Just right. I saw what it was. Grey sea –

MARION: Yes, you said. Gritty sand.

ALEC: It's just that I'd had a lot of difficulty. Wanting things. Or seeing no point in them. And since then I haven't.

MARION: Are we talking about a mystical experience? I've met people who've had those before. I knew a girl who thought she was Joan of Arc and kept setting fire to herself. When I hold up a grape – look at the grape – is it some blinding sort of – symbolic sort of – revelation that you get?

ALEC: No.

MARION: What is it then?

ALEC: A grape.

MARION: And what about me? What am I? What about me?

ALEC: There you are. I can't say. How can I? There you are.

(Pause.)

MARION: Are you staying here with your mother all night?

ALEC: No, I'll go home in a minute.

MARION: I wouldn't mind what you said you felt or didn't feel. If you do what I want and come away with me.

ALEC: How would that help?

MARION: What can I do to you? What do you care about? I'll find something. One day I'll have the pleasure of knowing you're screaming. Even if you do it silently.

(ALEC disconnects the drip.)

What are you doing? Don't touch that. Alec. What are you doing?

ALEC: There. That saves a lot of bother.

SCENE FOUR

ALEC and LISA in their room. LISA with hair and eyes again - she's back at work, but tired, wearing slippers.

LISA: I hate that black paint as you come up the stairs. Anyone who deliberately puts that on their walls can't be right. If they're all that keen on painting they could come and do some up here. Not her colour chart, I wouldn't have that. I'd choose my own colours.

ALEC: I'll paint it. What colour do you want?

LISA: He's the landlord isn't he? Let him keep it in good repair.

ALEC: It is in good repair. The damp's gone.

LISA: Then it's all ready for him to paint, isn't it.

ALEC: I thought you liked him.

LISA: Oh I do, I think he's lovely. So well spoken and well paid. His trousers are too tight.

ALEC: I'll get the paint Saturday morning then.

LISA: She's lovely too. Isn't she lovely?

ALEC: All right.

LISA: I'd be lovely in clothes like that.

ALEC: You are anyway.

LISA: That came a bit slow.

ALEC: Buy a new dress. It's a long time since you bought anything.

LISA: Just buying a dress wouldn't do it.

(Pause.)

I never thought I'd miss your mum, but she was company in a funny way.

(Pause.)

There's always been people like that. We just didn't live on top of them. Why do they have to leave their doors open? I don't want to see that kitchen all white and steel and everything in it the same height. No handles. Knives on a magnet just held to the wall. I don't want to know. And that enormous room just for a baby. Why should I have to see that every time I'm coming up with the shopping? I will not feed their bleeding cat while they're in Italy.

ALEC: I don't mind the cat. The boys like it.

(Pause.)

LISA: Alec I'm not going to get upset so you're not to stop me talking about it. Don't you miss the baby?

ALEC: I can't say I do, no. He's very well. It's not as if he's missing us.

LISA: I don't care if he's well or nearly dead. What good is it to me him being well in Marion's house? I want him here.

ALEC: You signed the papers.

LISA: How could I tell what I was doing? I wasn't in my right mind. I couldn't even see.

ALEC: It's done now.

LISA: Do something else, then, and get him back. What can we do? I think I might snatch him from the pram. Or even someone else's baby. I'd tell the police and the papers I'd give that woman's baby back if they got me my baby back. Why shouldn't I do something for once? Other people do all the things. Never me. I'm done things to.

ALEC: Shall we have another baby?

LISA: Another baby's got nothing to do with it. I'm getting this baby back home.

MRS ARLINGTON (calls off): Lisa? (Knock at door.) Lisa.

LISA: Coming.

(She doesn't stir. After a moment ALEC gets up and opens the door. MRS ARLINGTON comes in.)

MRS ARLINGTON: Oh thank you. I'm awfully sorry to disturb you. I was just saying I've fixed up the intercom so if she does wake up you should hear all right but I don't think she will because the last three nights she's actually slept through. Anyway I've left a bottle in the fridge so you'll only have to warm it up, and don't worry if she doesn't drink it all because I've made it a bit big so there's sure to be enough. And the nappies are in the airing cupboard. But as I say I don't think she'll wake before we're back and I hope not at all. We won't be later than one. Is that all right? You do look tired, Lisa. Go to bed early. I've got the volume switched up full so if she does cry she'll wake you up.

LISA: I always do go to bed early.

MRS ARLINGTON: Perhaps that's the trouble. You ought to go out more. I know I get terribly fed up if we don't go out a couple of times a week, and you're always babysitting for us and we gladly would for you but you never ask.

LISA: We never did go out very much. And once when we did for a couple of hours somebody broke in, which just shows. No, I don't believe in leaving children. You don't have them to leave them.

MRS ARLINGTON: If there's someone you can trust in the house –

LISA: I've never been in the habit of doing it.

MRS ARLINGTON: But one simply has to get out sometimes or one would go mad. I know I can trust you perfectly to look after Katie if she wakes up.

LISA: You wouldn't know if I didn't.

MRS ARLINGTON: Have you ever not gone to her? Have you left her crying? Have you?

LISA: She's never woke up yet.

MRS ARLINGTON: But what are you saying? Are you saying you'd leave her to cry?

ALEC: Of course she's not saying that. Go on and enjoy yourself.

MRS ARLINGTON: No but I'm not going till she promises she'll go to Katie the minute she hears her cry. To leave her half an hour or something like that could damage her mind for life.

ALEC: Go on, it's all right.

MRS ARLINGTON: No, not till she promises.

MR ARLINGTON (voice off): Penny!

MRS ARLINGTON: You're making us late for the theatre.

(Pause.)

All right, we won't go out.

LISA: I don't care what you do.

MR ARLINGTON (off): Penny!

ALEC: If the baby does wake up I'll go and see her.

MRS ARLINGTON: Are you sure?

ALEC: I wouldn't let Katie cry. Now go along.

MRS ARLINGTON: If it's really all right.

MR ARLINGTON (off): Penny!

(MRS ARLINGTON hesitates, then goes.)

ALEC: Cup of tea? I'll put the kettle on.

(He goes out to the landing.)

LISA: I'm not something that goes with the house.

(ALEC comes back.)

Right. I'm leaving.

ALEC: How do you mean?

LISA: I'm not staying here.

ALEC: You're leaving me and the boys? Or just me?

LISA: Leaving this place. Of course I'm not leaving the boys,
don't be stupid. They go wherever I go. And what's more
I'm getting the baby. I didn't mean leaving you but if you
won't come then I will leave you because I'm leaving here
and that's certain.

ALEC: I don't mind leaving here.

LISA: You can't live right in the same house with someone
and they've got everything and go out all the time.

ALEC: We can go out.

LISA: I don't want to go out. I don't want to live here with
them going out. I don't want to look like her and paint the
walls black. But I don't want to live in her house where
the walls should be black if it's her house and look at this
old wallpaper sitting here all night in my old dress.

ALEC: We'll have to find a place.

LISA: All right then we'll have to find a place. People do.
They're not all sleeping in the streets are they, you'd trip
over them. So they must all be somewhere. At least
you're earning again. What I do mind is we could have
had all that money to go and now we're doing the same
thing for nothing. Marion's going to have a good laugh.
But I don't want a corner in their house. They can have

their whole house for theirselves. Two black guest rooms.

(Pause while ALEC goes out and comes back with tray of tea.)

I don't see that signing a bit of paper makes him hers. He is mine. His blood and everything. His looks. His - everything he was born with, what he's like. Is yours and mine.

SCENE FIVE

CLEGG and LISA in Clegg's bed, him on top, bouncing up and down under the bedclothes.

CLEGG: An eye for an eye. A mouth for a mouth. A cunt for a cunt. Vengeance is mine. I will repay. In full.

(He collapses on her and lies still. After a moment LISA's head comes out from under the blanket.)

LISA: I only came to see the baby.

CLEGG: See him again after.

LISA: You will do all you can for me, won't you?

CLEGG: I just did. What do you want now?

LISA: The baby. You'll sort out the law, sort of thing.

CLEGG (lifts off her and rolls heavily over onto his back): I'm quite puffed. Unaccustomed exertion. They say it's like a five mile run. Or walk is it? Best way of keeping the tum down. Marion's fault I've lost my figure.

LISA: What shall I say to Alec?

CLEGG: Rub it in. Tell him just how marvellously good I was.

LISA: I don't know if I want to tell him at all.

CLEGG: What's the good of it if he never knows? I'll tell him myself. Let him just try and make a fuss. He doesn't know who he's dealing with. What have I had from him that he hasn't had from me? And he's still had most. I've plenty more owing. Plenty more where that came from.

LISA: I feel so funny. I think it must be guilty. Yes I'm sure it is. I felt the same when the headmaster found me behind the apparatus with Nutter Jones. He put his hand right inside my knickers. The headmaster, I mean, in his office. I felt in such a muddle and it all seemed to be my fault though I didn't see what I should have done to

make it happen different. And I don't see now. One thing
led to so many others. It wasn't really what was in my
mind. Nutter Jones came off his motor bike a few years
after and smashed his head. He should have worn a
helmet. It's always been Alec done it before. I've only
ever had to forgive him.

CLEGG: Your turn now. You've every right.

LISA: He's being ever so nice at the moment. Really normal.
A perfect husband and father. I'd hate to upset him. I
might not tell him about this. Just say I came to see you
and you gave me the baby.

CLEGG: No I didn't.

LISA: You will though.

CLEGG: Give you the baby?

LISA: That's what it was for.

CLEGG: What that was for? No it was not. It was my revenge.
A teeny little bit of my revenge.

LISA: We agreed before we started.

CLEGG: We did not.

LISA: Half way through then.

CLEGG: Nobody's responsible for what they say in the heat of
passion. If I had said at the time, I love you, you wouldn't
ever have thought I meant it. So if I said anything it's the
same. I don't remember us saying anything. Just heavy
breathing and mutters.

LISA: I want my baby.

CLEGG: He's my baby. Marion's bought him a shop.

LISA: Bought him a shop?

CLEGG: A brand new family butcher. Gold lettering. Clegg
and Son.

LISA: But he's _my_ son.

CLEGG: Lisa, listen to me. I didn't mean to hurt your feelings
when I said what I did was for revenge. I also thought what
a very sweet girl you are. I always did look at your
bottom in the old days. Nice bit of rump. Marion's more
like something for a stew. She's all gristle. But you melt
in the mouth.

LISA: You taste like a mouthful of sawdust off your floor. Look at you sweating like a bit of hot fat, which is what you are. With your belly sagging like a black pudding and your poor little pork sausage. Give me my baby.

CLEGG: It's not your nature to be offensive. I understand you being upset. Marion's enough to upset anyone. But if I was to give you the baby I wouldn't dare see her again. I don't care how angry you are, it's nothing like. With Marion it's like a mad person, you don't want to be in the same room, you don't want their attention to fall on you. It's not something I'd expose myself to.

LISA: I'll take him. You can say I took him and you couldn't stop me. She'll believe that. And it's true.

CLEGG: She'd have the police. Or she might commit a crime. She's very near some edge just now and I wouldn't want to push her off. In a mental sense. I don't trust her in a hospital, she takes advantage of the facilities. So just wait, I know a better way. A real solution. I'll admit I do get fed up with him though he is as nice a bit of little baby as you'll see. Turns the scales now at fifteen pounds, and I'm the one fattened him up and no one else. But when I start working again I'll have more important things to think about. A man can't be expected to stay home and look after a baby. He can do it of course because it's not difficult. Even a woman can do it easily. But it is a waste of real abilities.

LISA: I'll take him now.

CLEGG: He's Marion's and my little son, legally adopted. In some states of the United States the penalty for kidnapping is death. I think we can come to an arrangement. Some-one's got to look after the little sod while I'm at work, and you won't get Marion stopping home. So maybe, if you're very suitable – I'm not promising anything mind you – you could take care of him for us, on condition you see that he is still my son and will not be stopped by you from following his trade. Because I will not let that shiny new sign over my shop tell a lie.

LISA: So long as I have him.

CLEGG: We'll have to put it carefully to Marion. Where are you going?

LISA: I want to see him.

CLEGG: I didn't say you could get up. You won't be suitable unless you lie flat, did you know that, very feminine and do just as you're told. On your back and underneath is where I like to see a lady. And a man on top. Right on top of the world. Because I know what you ladies like. You like what I give you. I didn't say you mustn't move at all. But just in response.

SCENE SIX

Marion's office. ALEC alone. CLEGG comes in with the baby in a carrycot. When he sees ALEC he stops, then changes his mind and comes in firmly. At first a silence.

CLEGG: Some people think they're born lucky. Just walk through. Take what they like. Fall on their feet. I wouldn't count on finding a new flat without a great deal of effort and difficulty.

ALEC: I don't, no.

CLEGG: You say you don't, but you do. You think you can do what you like. You think everybody loves you just because one person is out of her mind. You're in for a very nasty shock.

ALEC: Housing is a problem, yes.

CLEGG: Lisa told you about our little plan? How we might let her mind our son part of the time? You've come to take part in the discussion. You feel an interest as the former father. Did she tell you where we talked it over?

ALEC: Yes.

CLEGG: In bed.

ALEC: Yes I can see how it might have happened. She is very upset about the baby.

CLEGG: She's told you, has she? She said she wouldn't. Woman's like that. Deceit is second nature. Due to Eve. But I'm too crafty for them by half. I know their ins and outs. You keep her rather short of it I'd say. Unless it was me that specially appealed to her. Yelping for more. I expect she told you. Or did she not bring out that side of it? I keep myself a little in reserve. You never know what else may turn up. I wouldn't want to waste myself on something as second rate as your wife. She was quite useful. A handy receptacle. But quite disposable after.

Isn't that your attitude to Marion?

ALEC: No.

CLEGG: You make a big mistake about Marion. She's not like other women in just one important respect. She is mine. I have invested heavily in Marion and don't intend to lose any part of my profit. She is my flesh. And touching her you touch me. And I will not let myself be touched.

(Pause.)

You pretend not to notice what I do to Lisa. I can do worse. And touching her I touch you. That's just one of the ways I'll be reaching you. You'll feel me. You'll come limb from limb for me one day. I'll think of you when I'm at work. Chop. Chop. Chop.

(WORSELY comes in. His wrists, neck and arm are still bandaged. His left leg is in plaster.)

ALEC: Hurt yourself?

WORSELY: I had a fall. I was climbing down at the time and I slipped.

CLEGG: Down what?

WORSELY: A fire escape.

CLEGG: Were you in a fire?

WORSELY: No. No.

CLEGG: Another time perhaps?

WORSELY: You never know.

CLEGG: I prefer a house that doesn't have any fire escape.

WORSELY: We'll have to talk about it some time. I think we're here to talk about the baby. I don't know why it's all dragged up again. The feelings involved make me quite sick.

CLEGG: How it came up was yesterday afternoon when I was having intercourse with his wife.

WORSELY: Lisa? You?

ALEC: Yes.

WORSELY (to ALEC): Tell me why you always act so calm.

CLEGG: He's pretending, to try and make me feel I don't matter, but I know I do.

WORSELY: Pretending? Are you?

ALEC: No.

WORSELY: He's not, you know. What he is, is nuts. I wonder
what it is Marion sees.

CLEGG: It soon won't matter what he's like. I can tell you
what Lisa sees in me.

WORSELY: I'm completely stunned she even looked at you.

CLEGG: Why?

WORSELY: No offence.

CLEGG: Why are you so stunned? She's not Miss World. She's
not even Miss South West Islington.

WORSELY: If I'd ever dreamt it was possible and without any
rucking from him I'd have had a try myself.

CLEGG: Be my guest.

WORSELY: It's her bottom.

CLEGG: It is definitely her bottom.

WORSELY: It's hard not to go in for this style of talk once
it's available. In fact I like Lisa. I feel quite shocked. Is
there really no row? Don't get me wrong. I don't like rows
very much. I can't stand anything very much. I'm not
looking forward to this discussion. It's going to get very
high pitched. My head's already aching from it. I don't
see why you had to bring the baby. It screws it all up that
much tighter. Something's got to snap. Have you had a
good look at Marion lately?

CLEGG: She's always very smart and does me credit.

WORSELY: She's not in a good state. (To ALEC:) Interested?

ALEC: I'm sorry to hear it.

WORSELY: You'd better be. She was all right. She was fine.
She was a success. Before you turned up again. I thought
I might punch you in the face but I don't think you'd notice.
And anyway I'd probably fall over. Have you ever tried
to kill yourself?

ALEC: No, I don't need to.

WORSELY: Are you dead already? I can't think how else you
avoid it. The thought of Marion alone is bad enough and it

should be worse for you.

CLEGG: I think it's my role not yours, Worsely, to worry about the state of my wife's health.

WORSELY: Worry, then.

CLEGG: Of course he doesn't need to kill himself. Most of us leave it to something or someone else.

WORSELY: I hear what you say.

CLEGG: You haven't forgotten our little arrangement? The central heating?

WORSELY: The central heating? Yes, that's good.

CLEGG: The financial side is taken care of. I've a cheque here made payable to T. Worsely. Signed Marion Clegg.

WORSELY: Didn't she ask why?

CLEGG: I think she'd better see a doctor.

WORSELY (taking the cheque): This is very welcome of course. But I'm not quite happy. I have some doubts.

CLEGG: I thought it was going ahead for tonight.

WORSELY: Can we talk about it some other time?

CLEGG: You said you had everything prepared.

WORSELY: I have, yes.

CLEGG: Then what's the problem? I'm counting on it, Worsely.

WORSELY: It's a great idea. There's nothing at all wrong with the idea. Except putting it into practice.

CLEGG: How dare you let me down? Give me the cheque. How dare you?

WORSELY (giving cheque back): I'm very brave.

CLEGG: You're a coward. A woman. A baby.

WORSELY: I didn't say I wouldn't. I'm just having a hesitation.

CLEGG: Then you'd better get moving again, sharpish.

WORSELY: I've too much on. I'm caving in. I owe a great deal to Marion and I don't altogether want to – do anything she'll disapprove of, however much she's – disappointed me.

CLEGG: I shouldn't come into my shop to be served, unless you have good news. With knives to hand the temptation might be irresistable for someone of my hot blooded disposition. I'm not in a mind for set backs. I had to have my dog put down.

WORSELY: Whatever for?

CLEGG: He bit me. I was teaching him a trick. I couldn't feel the same to him again. He made himself into just another animal.

(LISA comes in.)

LISA: Where is he? (She goes to the carrycot.) Can I pick him up?

CLEGG: He's asleep.

LISA: No, he's wakies, my little lamb. What blue blue eyes. Smile for mummy.

CLEGG: Better not. You don't want to get her against you from the start.

LISA: I'll put him down the minute she comes in.

CLEGG: I said leave him. What I like about you is you do what you're told.

WORSELY: You can pick him up later on, Lisa.

LISA: Oh what have you done now? Broken your leg. Were you skiing?

WORSELY: Not exactly, no.

LISA: I hope it doesn't hurt very much. Look at him smile.

WORSELY: When I talk to you it helps me forget the pain.

LISA: My grandmother was a Christian Scientist. Perhaps I've some power of healing. I've never seemed to have any before. I never seem to have any effect on anything. That's why you've got to help me get the baby because I know I can't manage Marion myself.

WORSELY: You can count on me. That's a lie. I wish my head – you haven't any aspirin?

LISA: How many?

WORSELY: Fifty would be nice.

LISA: Three. You will help me won't you? I know she listens

to what you say. And Clegg tells me you're really fond of
the baby.

WORSELY: The trouble is I'm getting fond of too many people.
I'm not against you. That much is clear.

(He turns away, is seized by CLEGG.)

CLEGG: We have a contract. I'll sue you for breach. We're
sworn to revenge. It's the next step. Oh, Worsely. First
him, then her. Then perfect peace.

LISA (to ALEC): We'll get the baby and get out of here, Alec,
we'll get far away and have a new life.

ALEC: We may do.

WORSELY: Oh, if my head would stop drumming.

(MARION comes in.)

MARION: I know my own mind. The legal position is perfectly
clear. What can there possibly be to discuss? I won't have
tears, Lisa. Clegg and I are united as the child's parents
in our opposition to any interference. Worsely will say
the same. You can't pretend Alec wants the baby. It is
just your hysteria, Lisa, against the reasonableness of
the rest of us.

LISA: I'm not crying this time. Too bad for you. I can see
what I'm doing this time.

MARION: Won't you take her home? I have work to do.

LISA: Alec and I both want him. It's just a game to you,
Marion. You don't want him really. You just want to win.

MARION: He's legally my child. His name is Clegg.

LISA: But I'm sure it can't really be the law. Can't we go to
a court and tell them I didn't know what I was signing?

MARION: It would take a lot of time. A lot of money. Meanwhile he's used to us and our home. Have you a home
that would impress a judge?

LISA: You're only doing it to be cruel to me. Why should you?
How can you?

MARION: I shall do as I like. Worsely, please make them all
go away.

CLEGG: But Marion, my dear, wait a moment. I'm sure we

can come to some arrangement.

MARION: Why should we? We've nothing to gain.

CLEGG: I can't look after him properly in the shop. Suppose we employ Lisa as a daily help to look after him while we're at work.

LISA: In my own home. I'd want him in my own home.

CLEGG: Provided you register with the council as an official babyminder.

MARION: Are you mad, Clegg? Giving him away? Once she's got her hands on him he won't be ours any more. You'll lose your little butcher.

CLEGG: I don't want that. We'd have to have a written agreement about his future.

MARION: There are plenty of people to look after babies. He will have a trained nanny.

CLEGG: But Lisa –

MARION: I said he will have a nanny. Are you going against me, Clegg? It was entirely for you I got the baby. I bought him a shop, for you. If you don't like the arrangements you can go. Clear right off. It would be a delight never to see you again.

LISA: I went to bed with him yesterday afternoon.

MARION: Is she mad?

CLEGG: Well what happened, in a manner of speaking –

MARION: I don't know which of you I'm most sorry for. Perhaps you'd like to take Lisa and the baby and set up house together, Clegg? I'm sure Alec and I wouldn't mind.

CLEGG: No of course I don't want that. It was just –

MARION: Then don't waste my time. Lisa doesn't come into our plans at all.

LISA: Don't let her frighten you Clegg.

MARION: Worsely, please, clear them all out.

WORSELY: One thing, Marion, perhaps...

MARION: Go on.

WORSELY: I don't like to contradict you...

MARION: What?

WORSELY: It might be better for the baby. If it was to go back to Lisa. Entirely.

MARION: Better for the baby? Why?

WORSELY: I don't think you like him very much.

MARION: I adore him.

CLEGG: I'm rather fond of the little chap myself. I wouldn't want to completely give him up.

WORSELY: I like him. More than Clegg does. Far more than you do, Marion. But I'm not saying that makes him mine. Let him go back where he belongs. You're letting yourself go mad, Marion. I've seen you in pieces. I don't know whether I want to smash you up or keep you safe. But you won't get Alec like this. You'll just damage the baby. Keep going, be a success, make a fortune. Use me for anything you like. You can still be magnificent.

(He bursts into tears.)

MARION: I think everyone's had their say. None of you has any effect on me.

(LISA picks up the carrycot and tries to rush out of the door. CLEGG grabs her, and they struggle briefly. He gets the carrycot and shuts the door.)

I think I'm going to send for the police.

CLEGG: The advantage of having Lisa to mind the baby is that if anything should happen to you, his mother, he would have you could say another mother in Lisa, which a nanny how-ever trained could never be.

MARION: Why should anything happen to me Clegg? More than to anyone else?

CLEGG: I must have second sight, Marion. I see you dead within a few weeks.

LISA: Oh what else can I do? Alec.

ALEC: I should like him back.

MARION: Say it again.

ALEC: I should like him back.

MARION: Again.

ALEC: No.

MARION: You'd like him back. Have you actually got a feeling? Put it under glass and it might grow. Wouldn't a different baby be just the same? Do you really mean you prefer your own baby? Next thing we know you'll say you prefer Lisa to me. Or me to Lisa. There's no telling what you might say once you start saying you want something.

ALEC: I should like him back. I can do without.

MARION: I can't do without. He's my bit of you. Not a bit of me. That doesn't matter. Not a bit of Clegg, thank God. But a bit of you.

ALEC: We're leaving the flat.

MARION: Leaving?

ALEC: Leaving London.

MARION: Leaving London?

ALEC: So let us go and take the baby with us.

MARION: Up till now, right up till now, I might have let you have the baby. What is it to me? But if you go it's all I'll have left.

LISA: If you let me mind the baby, Marion, in my own home, we would stay in London for that.

MARION: No. No no no. Very clever but I won't be caught. Leave me if you like but you won't get the baby. I will keep what's mine. The more you want it the more it's worth keeping. But you can't just go like that. I haven't paid you to go. Every one of you thinks I will give in. Because I'm a woman, is it? I'm meant to be kind. I'm meant to understand a woman's feelings wanting her baby back. I don't. I won't. I can be as terrible as anyone. Soldiers have stuck swords through innocents. I can massacre too. Into the furnace. Why shouldn't I be Genghis Khan? Empires only come by killing. I won't shrink. Not one of you loves me. But he shall grow up to say he does.

SCENE SEVEN

Office, later. WORSELY and MARION. The carrycot is on the floor near the door.

WORSELY: I was up on this very high ledge. You could get across to it from the fire escape. Even with one hand. So

there I was. If I had jumped it could only have been fatal.
Barring accidents. And what could have intercepted me?
If I'd hit a pigeon on the way down I'd have smashed it
down with me. A high building. So I sat there with a great
easing of misery because it was all so possible. A crowd
gathered, and so on. Sirens. I took no notice. It was
every moment in my power – on or off, be or not. And
then there turned up beside me of all people that Samaritan
friend. I think I've mentioned him. Very on-going. I'd
made a new will in his favour because I thought he always
meant well and put in a good deal of effort. B plus. He'd
come up on the ledge to squat beside me and talk me down.
We had a chat. Just this and that. I was just about to drop
off, suddenly, in the middle of what I was saying, to take
him by surprise, when I saw he had turned quite pale.
He can't have had much of a head for heights. And the
next thing, he'd gone. I was quite right to think the distance
would be fatal.

MARION: What about your leg?

WORSELY: I was climbing down the fire escape and I slipped.
I must have fallen about six feet and landed with my leg
sort of twisted. It was quite painful.

MARION: Worsely, could you do something for me? Something to hurt Alec.

WORSELY: Like what?

MARION: Think of something.

WORSELY: Fatal?

MARION: I wouldn't mind.

(Pause.)

WORSELY: Like set the house on fire?

(Pause.)

MARION: What a good idea. What a very nice thought.

(WORSELY gets up and goes to the door.)

WORSELY: I may meet my own death in the blaze.

(MARION doesn't react at all. WORSELY waits a moment,
then, unnoticed, picks up the carrycot and goes out with
it.)

SCENE EIGHT

CLEGG's new butcher's shop. CLEGG and CUSTOMER.

CLEGG: Nice chicken, won't keep you a moment. (He takes
a chicken and cutting off its head cleans it while he talks.)
Lovely day, dear, been in the park? Wish I could get away
myself and have the lazy day you housewives have. Giblets
dear? Shame to waste them. Eighty-five p altogether
darling. Ninety, one hundred. Thank you very much, good
morning.

(Customer goes out. MARION comes in.)

Slept in the office did you? You look like it. By yourself?
Take a bit more pride in your appearance, Marion, it's
slipping again.

MARION: You haven't seen Worsely? He hasn't come into the
office. I've left him a note. I've come up here.

CLEGG: What did you do for a bottle then?

MARION: Bottle?

CLEGG: I thought you'd come home with him later. Did you
have to go out and buy him one? Still it never hurts to have
a spare.

MARION: What are you talking about?

CLEGG: Baby Clegg of course, do wake up.

MARION: I haven't got him.

CLEGG: Of course you've got him.

MARION: Where?

CLEGG: Marion, what do you mean? I left him with you at the
office.

MARION: I thought he was at home with you.

CLEGG: You insisted I leave him there. Mine, you kept saying,
mine, don't you remember? Where is he?

MARION: In the office?

CLEGG: Is he in the office?

MARION: I seem to remember you did leave him, yes.

CLEGG: Didn't you feed him? All night? Didn't he cry?

MARION: He never cried. I never heard him cry.

CLEGG: Marion, you've let him starve to death.

MARION: I haven't. He wouldn't. He'd cry if he was hungry.

CLEGG: He must have cried.

MARION: I'll go back.

CLEGG: I'll go. You can't be trusted.

(WORSELY comes in. His face is partly bandaged from a burn. Other bandages and plaster as before.)

WORSELY: Alec's dead.

CLEGG: How?

MARION: In the fire?

CLEGG: You didn't do the fire after all? And killed him?

MARION: It was my idea.

CLEGG: It was mine, but I never thought it would come to this. Let's shut the shop.

MARION: Is he dead?

WORSELY: I got a few burns myself.

CLEGG: No one can say it was me. You assured me you were not going to do it, Worsely. I never even gave you the cheque.

MARION: It was me. I asked Worsely to do something to Alec. He chose fire.

CLEGG: Did you? Did she? You amaze me. And meanwhile she's lost the baby.

WORSELY: I took him to Lisa.

MARION: What? When did you?

WORSELY: When I left yesterday evening. You weren't looking. I bet you never thought did you, till today? He's not your baby, Marion, by any stretch of the imagination. I delivered him to Lisa anyway. She was very glad. So was Alec. The Arlingtons were out as it happened. So on the way down I did my bit with the petrol in their sitting room. Very tasteful trendy furnishings altogether.

CLEGG: You gave my baby butcher away?

WORSELY: What worried me a little I must say was the thought of the baby in the fire. Since I'd gone to the trouble of

bringing him round. So after I'd gone down to the street
and seen it get started I went back in and shouted Fire,
fire. The stairs were already aflame so none too soon.
But in no time they were all rushing down, Lisa shrieking
as you can imagine, her hair singeing, Alec with the baby,
the boys stumbling hanging on her hands, and all of them
shot out onto the pavement.

MARION: But Alec?

WORSELY: At this point I thought myself of going back in.
Fire has a terrible attraction. As it leaps and licks up,
like a creature taking over, when really of course it was
the house turning into fire because of the high temperature
it was reaching rather than a fire consuming the house.
Strictly speaking. I went back in through the front door.
It was very hot. I went on. It was smoky so I couldn't
properly see. I went on, you must give me marks for
perseverance, and no, I certainly can't kill myself by fire,
it is far too hot.

MARION: But what about Alec?

WORSELY: I was just coming out, and meanwhile I heard the
fire engines, when Alec came in through the door, walking
quite calmly considering the heat. 'The other baby, you
see' is what he said and set off – I would say up the stairs
but I couldn't exactly see them in the flames. But he rose
as if climbing the stairs. Turning into fire quite silently.
We waited but of course he didn't come out and nor did
the Arlingtons' baby. It was too hot.

CLEGG: The grand climax of my revenge was to be shooting
you, Marion, here in the shop. Every woman wants to be
loved like that. It's more than he would ever have done.
Look, here in the drawer is the murder weapon. But now
he's gone, and you wanted him gone, wanted the same
thing I wanted, we are one again. I forgive you everything.
If the police come, say nothing. Leave it all to me. I
certainly never intended such a shocking fatal accident as
that, and I'm sure you didn't. I will protect you.

MARION: I'm not sorry at all about Alec. Or about that other
baby. Not at all. I never knew I could do a thing like that.
I might be capable of anything. I'm just beginning to find
out what's possible.

(WORSELY picks up the gun and takes up a stance, placing
it by his temple. He fires.)

WORSELY: Missed.

Other Methuen Playscripts

Methuen's Modern Plays

Edited by John Cullen and Geoffrey Strachan

	THE GOOD PERSON OF SZECHWAN
	THE LIFE OF GALILEO
Syd Cheatle	STRAIGHT UP
Shelagh Delaney	A TASTE OF HONEY
	THE LION IN LOVE
Max Frisch	THE FIRE RAISERS
	ANDORRA
Jean Giraudoux	TIGER AT THE GATES
Simon Gray	SPOILED
	BUTLEY
Peter Handke	OFFENDING THE AUDIENCE and
	SELF ACCUSATION
	KASPAR
Rolf Hochhuth	THE REPRESENTATIVE
Heinar Kipphardt	IN THE MATTER OF J. ROBERT
	OPPENHEIMER
Arthur Kopit	CHAMBER MUSIC and OTHER PLAYS
	INDIANS
Jakov Lind	THE SILVER FOXES ARE DEAD
	and OTHER PLAYS
David Mercer	ON THE EVE OF PUBLICATION
	AFTER HAGGERTY
	FLINT
John Mortimer	THE JUDGE
	FIVE PLAYS
	COME AS YOU ARE
	A VOYAGE ROUND MY FATHER
Joe Orton	CRIMES OF PASSION
	LOOT
	WHAT THE BUTLER SAW
	FUNERAL GAMES and THE GOOD AND
	FAITHFUL SERVANT
Harold Pinter	THE BIRTHDAY PARTY
	THE ROOM and THE DUMB WAITER
	THE CARETAKER
	A SLIGHT ACHE and OTHER PLAYS
	THE COLLECTION and THE LOVER
	THE HOMECOMING
	TEA PARTY and OTHER PLAYS
	LANDSCAPE AND SILENCE
	OLD TIMES
David Selbourne	THE DAMNED
Jean-Paul Sartre	CRIME PASSIONNEL
Wole Soyinka	MADMEN AND SPECIALISTS
	THE JERO PLAYS
Boris Vian	THE EMPIRE BUILDERS
Peter Weiss	TROTSKY IN EXILE

Theatre Workshop and Charles Chilton	OH WHAT A LOVELY WAR
Charles Wood	'H'
	VETERANS
Carl Zuckmayer	THE CAPTAIN OF KOPENICK

If you would like regular information
on new Methuen plays, please write to
The Marketing Department
Eyre Methuen Ltd
11 New Fetter Lane
London EC4P 4EE